I0006005

THE FUTURE OF MONEY AND FINANCE

HOW CRYPTO AND WEB3 ARE CHANGING THE GAME

The future of money is here, and it belongs to you! Discover the groundbreaking technologies of cryptocurrency and Web3 that are revolutionizing finance as we know it. Learn how blockchain, decentralized applications (DApps), and DAOs are shifting power away from banks and tech giants back into the hands of individuals. Explore how you can participate in this financial transformation, create new opportunities, and gain greater control over your financial destiny.

CHAPTER 1:

The Evolution of Money

From seashells to smartphones, the way we exchange value has undergone a fascinating journey. Understanding this evolution sets the stage for exploring how cryptocurrency and Web3 are poised to revolutionize the very concept of money.

From Bartering to Banking

In the earliest societies, goods were exchanged directly. A farmer might trade a bushel of wheat for a pair of shoes crafted by a skilled artisan. This system, called bartering, was simple but had limitations. What if the farmer didn't need shoes, or the shoemaker had no use for wheat? Necessity drove the invention of early currencies.

Precious metals like gold and silver became popular mediums of exchange. They were durable, easily divisible, and held intrinsic value that most people agreed upon. Coins standardized transactions, but carrying heavy pouches of metal wasn't ideal. Eventually, paper money emerged, backed by promises from governments and banks. This shift marked a transition toward trust-based systems.

The Rise of Digital Money

With the advent of the internet, digital currencies were inevitable. Electronic payments, like credit and debit cards, sped up transactions but still relied on centralized banks. These systems, while convenient, have inherent limitations. They can be slow (especially across borders), expensive due to fees, and vulnerable to the control of institutions or governments.

The Need for Something New

Traditional banks and financial systems, developed centuries ago, aren't perfectly suited for a globalized, interconnected world. Many people remain unbanked or underserved by these legacy institutions. Financial crises have eroded trust. The time is ripe for a new paradigm in how we think about and interact with money.

Enter Cryptocurrency: A Digital Revolution

Cryptocurrency, born from a desire to bypass traditional financial systems, leverages the power of blockchain technology. A blockchain is like a shared, unchangeable public ledger that records transactions securely. This technology eliminates the need for central intermediaries like banks.

Bitcoin, introduced in 2009, blazed the trail for a new era of digital money. With Bitcoin, individuals can directly transact with each other without needing permission from a third party. Cryptocurrencies offer several potential advantages over traditional money:

- **Decentralization:** No single authority controls the network, making it resistant to censorship or manipulation.
- **Borderless:** Transactions can happen across the globe almost instantly, without the limitations of national currencies.
- **Transparency:** While users remain pseudo-anonymous, every transaction is recorded on the public blockchain.
- **Programmability:** Cryptocurrencies can be used for more than just payments due to their integration with smart contracts (self-executing code on the blockchain).

A New Era of Financial Possibility

Cryptocurrency may seem complex, but its potential impact is profound. It represents a fundamental shift in the concept of money: a system where trust is built into the technology itself, not reliant on institutions. While still in its early stages, cryptocurrency has the potential to redefine the way we save, spend, invest, and even think about the value of money.

CHAPTER 2:

Cryptocurrency: The Foundation of a New Financial System

In the previous chapter, we explored the evolutionary journey of money. Now, it's time to understand the mechanics behind cryptocurrencies, the digital assets driving the financial revolution. We'll uncover the backbone of this innovation: blockchain technology.

The Magic of Blockchain

Imagine a giant digital ledger that is continuously updated and shared across thousands of computers worldwide. This is the essence of blockchain technology. Each transaction is time-stamped and bundled into a "block" that is linked to the previous block with a cryptographic code, like a fingerprint. This chain of blocks becomes nearly impossible to alter retroactively.

Here's why blockchain technology is so powerful for cryptocurrencies:

- **Decentralization:** No central server exists. The network relies on the combined power of its participants, making it resistant to tampering or shutdowns.
- **Transparency:** All transactions are visible on the public ledger (although user identities remain hidden), promoting accountability.
- **Immutability:** Once a transaction is recorded in a block, it cannot be easily altered, reducing fraud and disputes.

The Power of Cryptography

Blockchain relies on complex cryptography, essentially a way of safeguarding information through mathematical codes. Cryptocurrencies use cryptographic keys, think of them as ultra-secure passwords. These keys enable you to sign transactions on the blockchain, proving ownership of your coins without revealing your identity.

Mining: The Backbone of Many Cryptocurrencies

Many cryptocurrencies, including Bitcoin, use a process called "mining" to secure the network and create new coins. Miners are powerful computers that race to solve intricate mathematical puzzles. The first to solve the puzzle gets to add the next block to the blockchain and earns cryptocurrency as a reward. This process incentivizes people to support the network and creates scarcity for the cryptocurrency.

Key Properties of Cryptocurrencies

Beyond the underlying blockchain technology, cryptocurrencies possess several unique characteristics that differentiate them from traditional money:

- **Limited Supply:** Many cryptocurrencies like Bitcoin have a hard cap on the total number of coins that will ever exist. This creates built-in scarcity, unlike fiat currencies where governments can print more money at will.
- **Divisibility:** Cryptocurrencies can be broken down into tiny fractions. For instance, you can buy 0.00001 Bitcoin, making it accessible for investments of any size.
- **Borderless Nature:** Cryptocurrencies operate independently of national borders. Sending crypto internationally can be as fast and easy as sending it to a neighbor.
- **Pseudonymity:** While transactions are recorded on the public blockchain, your personal identity isn't directly linked. You interact using wallet addresses – strings of

numbers and letters.

Beyond Bitcoin

While Bitcoin pioneered the cryptocurrency landscape, it's far from the only player. Thousands of other cryptocurrencies, often called altcoins, have emerged. Some, like Ethereum, offer expanded functionality, enabling the creation of decentralized applications and smart contracts, revolutionizing whole industries.

Other cryptocurrencies focus on different niches:

- **Privacy coins:** Aim to enhance anonymity and untraceable transactions.
- **Stablecoins:** Designed to peg their value to an underlying asset like the US dollar, minimizing volatility.
- **Meme coins:** Often inspired by internet memes, their value is largely driven by community sentiment.

A World of Possibilities

The world of cryptocurrency is ever-evolving, offering new possibilities across various sectors. While Bitcoin sparked the movement as digital gold, the technology's potential reaches far beyond simple currency replacements.

CHAPTER 3:

Web3: Reimagining the Internet

The internet has undeniably transformed how we communicate, learn, and do business. However, today's web is largely dominated by a handful of tech giants that centralize data, limit user control, and profit from our online activity. Web3 aims to break this model, empowering individuals and ushering in a new era of the decentralized web.

The Evolution of the Web

Let's take a brief look at the web's journey to understand why Web3 is gaining traction:

- **Web1 (Read-Only Web):** The early web was mostly static pages with limited interactivity. Think of it as a giant online encyclopedia.
- **Web2 (Participatory Web):** The rise of social media, user-generated content, and e-commerce marked Web2. While it allowed greater interaction, it also led to increased centralization of power in the hands of a few platforms.
- **Web3 (Ownership Web):** Web3 aims to distribute power back to individuals by leveraging blockchain, cryptocurrencies, and decentralized technologies. It promises a web where users own their data, directly participate in governance, and reap the rewards of their contributions.

Key Components of Web3

Web3 isn't simply one technology but a collection of principles and technologies that enable the shift towards decentralization:

- **DApps (Decentralized Applications):** Unlike traditional apps that run on centralized servers, DApps operate on a blockchain network. This means no single entity can control the application or user data.
- **DAOs (Decentralized Autonomous Organizations):** Think of them as internet-native organizations governed by smart contracts and community voting. DAOs offer a transparent and democratic way to manage projects or communities.
- **Tokenized Economies:** Cryptocurrencies and tokens power Web3, enabling users to directly own and trade digital assets within decentralized platforms. This opens new models for creators to monetize their work and communities to reward members.

How Web3 Empowers Individuals

In contrast to Web2, where platforms often extract value from users, Web3 envisions a user-centric paradigm. This shift has profound implications:

- **Ownership of Data:** Instead of your data being a commodity for tech giants, Web3 gives you control. You can selectively decide what information to share and potentially even profit from it.
- **Direct Participation:** Web3 platforms often incorporate governance tokens. Holding these tokens gives users voting rights, allowing them to shape the direction and rules of the platform.
- **True Digital Ownership:** The introduction of NFTs (Non-Fungible Tokens) on the blockchain ensures verifiable proof of ownership for digital assets like art, music, and in-game items. Artists and creators can directly connect with fans without intermediaries.

- **Censorship Resistance:** Decentralized architecture makes Web3 applications less susceptible to censorship or shutdowns by a single authority.

Web3 in Action

While Web3 is still developing, we're starting to see its principles applied in various ways:

- **Decentralized Social Media:** Platforms aiming to give users control over content moderation and allow them to earn rewards for their contributions.
- **Web3 Gaming:** Games where players truly own their in-game assets as NFTs, enabling them to be traded or even used across different platforms.
- **Decentralized Marketplaces:** Open platforms for buying and selling goods and services using cryptocurrencies, without relying on centralized platforms like Amazon or eBay.

The Road to Mass Adoption

Web3 holds the potential to transform numerous industries, yet it faces several challenges before reaching widespread adoption. These include scalability issues, lack of user-friendly interfaces, and the complexity of managing your own digital assets.

CHAPTER 4:

Disrupting Banking and Payments

Traditional banking systems have served their purpose for centuries. However, their limitations are becoming increasingly apparent in a globalized and digital world. Cryptocurrencies and Web3 are poised to revolutionize the way we send, receive, and interact with money.

Unlocking Faster, Cheaper Payments

Cryptocurrencies offer several advantages over traditional payment systems when it comes to international remittances. Sending money across borders has long been a slow, expensive process due to multiple intermediaries involved in the process.

Here's how cryptocurrencies make a difference:

- **Reduced Fees:** Blockchain transactions generally cost a fraction of what banks or services like Western Union charge.
- **Near-Instant Transfers:** Crypto transactions clear within minutes or even seconds, regardless of location. Unlike wire transfers that can take days.
- **Accessibility:** Cryptocurrency transfers only require an internet connection and a crypto wallet, making them accessible even in areas with limited banking infrastructure.

Financial Inclusion for the Underserved

Billions of people around the world are "unbanked," meaning they have no access to traditional financial services. Cryptocurrencies offer an alternative gateway to participating in the global economy. All it takes is a smartphone and an internet connection to send, receive, and even save digital currencies.

Micropayments and New Business Models

The fees associated with traditional payment systems make micropayments (tiny transactions) often impractical. Cryptocurrencies, with their low transaction costs, open up possibilities such as:

- **Pay-per-article content:** Directly supporting creators without subscriptions.
- **Machine-to-machine payments:** Enabling the "Internet of Things" economy where devices can transact autonomously.
- **Tipping and donations:** Rewarding content creators or supporting causes with even small amounts.

Challenges for Traditional Banking

The benefits offered by cryptocurrencies pose a potential threat to traditional banks and financial institutions. If people can easily access fast, affordable, and borderless payment systems without needing conventional banks, what will the role of these institutions be?

- **Loss of Revenue:** If a significant portion of transactions shifts to the blockchain, banks could lose profits from fees and foreign exchange.
- **Disintermediation:** Web3 enables peer-to-peer transactions and services, reducing the need for banks as middlemen.
- **Innovation Pressure:** Crypto and Web3 are forcing banks to innovate and adopt new technologies or risk being left

behind.

Stablecoins: A Bridge Between Worlds

Stablecoins are a type of cryptocurrency designed to maintain a stable value, usually pegged to a fiat currency like the US dollar. They offer some benefits of traditional currencies with the speed and efficiency of the blockchain.

Stablecoins play an important role in mitigating volatility, which is a significant barrier for broader cryptocurrency adoption. They serve as a bridge, allowing easier transitions between fiat and crypto, providing a familiar entry point for those new to the space.

The Future of Payments

It's likely that both traditional banking and Web3 payment systems will coexist, each catering to different needs. Banks with a long history of trust and compliance may still be preferred for large transactions and government-related interactions. Cryptocurrencies and blockchain solutions will continue to revolutionize areas like remittances, micro-transactions, and opening up opportunities for the unbanked.

CHAPTER 5:

The Rise of Decentralized Finance (DeFi)

Cryptocurrencies opened the gate to decentralized payments. DeFi takes this concept to the next level. It aims to recreate traditional financial services like lending, borrowing, trading, insurance, and more – without the control of banks or other centralized institutions.

DeFi Building Blocks

DeFi is built upon the following foundational components:

- **Smart Contracts:** These self-executing contracts on the blockchain automate financial agreements. They eliminate the need for intermediaries, reducing costs and increasing efficiency.
- **Cryptocurrencies:** DeFi applications primarily utilize cryptocurrencies (often Ethereum), enabling these decentralized services to exist.
- **DApps:** Decentralized applications built on the blockchain power the DeFi ecosystem, allowing users to interact with various financial protocols.

Beyond Speculation: Real-World Applications of DeFi

While early cryptocurrency use-cases focused on trading and speculation, DeFi offers a vast array of practical applications:

- **Lending and Borrowing:** Platforms allow individuals

to lend their cryptocurrency and earn interest, or borrow crypto using other coins as collateral.

- **Decentralized Exchanges (DEXs):** These platforms enable users to trade cryptocurrencies directly with each other, without a centralized exchange taking custody of funds.
- **Yield Farming:** A high-risk, high-reward strategy where users provide liquidity to DeFi protocols and earn rewards in the form of new tokens.
- **Insurance:** Decentralized insurance platforms offer protection against risks associated with smart contracts and DeFi protocols.

Democratizing Financial Services

DeFi's potential impact is vast. It promises to:

- **Lower barriers to entry:** Individuals don't need credit checks or extensive paperwork to access financial services, opening up opportunities globally.
- **Increase transparency:** Smart contracts operate transparently on the blockchain, increasing accountability and reducing the risk of fraudulent activity.
- **Provide new investment options:** DeFi opens up novel ways to earn interest, access loans, and participate in more complex financial instruments.

Risks and Challenges in the DeFi Landscape

While offering exciting possibilities, DeFi is still in its early stages and comes with potential risks that users should be aware of:

- **Smart Contract Bugs:** Complex code that powers DeFi platforms can contain vulnerabilities. Hacks and exploits have resulted in significant financial losses.
- **Volatility:** Cryptocurrency prices can be volatile, which is

especially risky in DeFi applications where loans are often collateralized with crypto assets.

- **Lack of Regulation:** Currently, the DeFi space is largely unregulated. This poses risks of scams and offers limited recourse for users in case of fraud or disputes.
- **User Complexity:** Navigating the DeFi ecosystem requires a degree of technical understanding. It can be intimidating for beginners, leading to mistakes and potential loss of funds.

The Road to Mass Adoption

For DeFi to reach its full potential, these challenges need to be addressed:

- **Security Improvements:** Smart contract audits, code reviews, and insurance solutions can mitigate the risk of exploits and offer some protection to users.
- **Clear Regulations:** Sensible regulation could foster innovation while protecting users and preventing fraudulent activity.
- **User-Friendly Interfaces:** Simplifying access to DeFi applications will be critical for wider adoption.

CHAPTER 6:

DAOs: A New Model of Governance and Ownership

Decentralized Autonomous Organizations (DAOs) are redefining how groups collaborate and make decisions. Think of them as internet-native organizations where power and control are distributed among members instead of being held by a central leader or hierarchy.

How DAOs Work

The foundation of any DAO is a set of rules encoded as smart contracts on a blockchain. These smart contracts define how the organization will function. Here's a simplified explanation of how DAOs operate:

- **Collective Decision-Making:** Members of a DAO typically hold governance tokens that represent voting rights. Proposals for actions – whether it's funding a project or changing internal rules – are put to a vote.
- **Transparency and Immutability:** Every vote and transaction within the DAO is recorded on the public blockchain. This ensures transparency and makes it difficult for individuals to manipulate the system.
- **Autonomous Execution:** Once a proposal reaches the required consensus, the smart contract automatically carries out the decision. This eliminates the need for intermediaries or reliance on human action.

Types of DAOs

DAOs come in numerous shapes and sizes, serving a variety of purposes:

- **Investment DAOs:** Pools of capital controlled by members who collectively invest in various projects or assets.
- **Protocol DAOs:** Communities that govern the development and maintenance of decentralized platforms or applications.
- **Social DAOs:** Formed around shared interests, social clubs, or online communities that align with a common goal.
- **Collector DAOs:** Collaboratively purchase and manage valuable items, such as NFTs or digital artwork.
- **Philanthropic DAOs:** Dedicated to funding charitable causes or supporting social impact projects.

The Potential of DAOs

DAOs offer a groundbreaking approach to collaboration, ownership, and decision-making. Their potential benefits include:

- **Democratization:** DAOs empower every member to have a voice and influence an organization's direction.
- **Efficiency:** Decisions can be executed swiftly and automatically once they meet the set voting thresholds.
- **Global Participation:** DAOs operate borderlessly, allowing members from around the world to collaborate.

Examples of Real-World DAOs

DAOs are already operating in diverse sectors. Here are a few notable examples:

- **MakerDAO:** One of the largest and longest-running DAOs, governs the development of the DAI stablecoin and manages its lending protocol.

- **Uniswap:** A popular decentralized exchange (DEX) governed by holders of the UNI governance token.
- **PleasrDAO:** A collector DAO focused on acquiring culturally significant NFTs and promoting their accessibility.
- **KlimaDAO:** A DAO dedicated to combating climate change by incentivizing and purchasing carbon assets.

Challenges and Considerations

While DAOs offer a promising future, they also face hurdles to widespread adoption:

- **Legal and Regulatory Uncertainty:** The legal status of DAOs is still evolving, making it unclear how they'll be treated within existing legal frameworks.
- **Technical Complexity:** Effectively participating in a DAO can require a degree of technical understanding, which might act as a barrier for some.
- **Scalability and Decision-Making:** As DAOs grow, finding efficient ways to make decisions while ensuring broad participation can be challenging.
- **Security Risks:** Smart contracts, as with any code, can have vulnerabilities that hackers could exploit.

The Future of Governance

DAOs represent a transformative paradigm shift in how we think about organizations. They offer the potential to foster more inclusive, transparent, and efficient forms of collaboration on a global scale. As the technology and regulatory landscape matures, we can expect to see DAOs playing an increasingly important role in industries ranging from finance to social impact and beyond.

Conclusion:

The Future of Finance Belongs to the People

Throughout this book, we've embarked on a journey through the evolution of money, the technology underpinning cryptocurrencies, the emergence of Web3, and the disruption of financial systems. A central theme has emerged: power is shifting from institutions back to individuals.

Cryptocurrency, built on the foundation of blockchain technology, offers a trust-less, transparent, and decentralized alternative to traditional money. Web3 envisions a user-centric internet where communities directly own and govern platforms, utilizing tokens to incentivize participation and reward creators. DeFi is building the infrastructure for a new global financial system, more accessible and democratic than its predecessor. And DAOs are pioneering models of collaboration where stakeholders collectively shape the future of organizations and communities.

While these technologies are still in their nascent stages, their potential impact is undeniable:

- **Financial inclusion:** Expanding access to financial services for the underserved, opening up new economic opportunities globally.
- **Innovation and Competition:** Web3 forces traditional financial institutions to adapt and innovate, ultimately making the system better for users.
- **Ownership and Empowerment:** Individuals gain greater control over their data, assets, and participation in digital economies.

Challenges and Opportunities

The path ahead will have its hurdles. Smart contracts need stronger security, user experiences must be simplified, and regulations will evolve to strike a balance between innovation and consumer protection. Education plays a vital role. As individuals better understand the technology and its potentials, informed choices will drive responsible adoption

The Era of Decentralization

We are witnessing a paradigm shift in how we interact with money, finance, and the internet itself. The future is likely to be a hybrid one, where traditional systems coexist with decentralized solutions. Those who embrace these changes will likely find themselves at the forefront of a financial revolution.

Cryptocurrency and Web3 technologies have the potential to level the playing field, unlock global potential, and create a more equitable financial system. The power to shape this future lies not just in the hands of developers and corporations, but in the hands of each individual who chooses to be part of this evolving landscape.

GLOSSARY

- **Altcoin:** Any cryptocurrency other than Bitcoin.

- **Blockchain:** A decentralized, distributed digital ledger that records transactions securely and transparently across a network of computers.

- **Cold Wallet:** A type of cryptocurrency wallet that stores private keys offline for enhanced security.

- **Consensus Mechanism:** The method a blockchain network uses to reach agreement on the validity of transactions and the shared state of the ledger. Examples include Proof-of-Work (PoW) and Proof-of-Stake (PoS).

- **Cryptocurrency:** A digital or virtual currency that uses cryptography for security and operates independently of a central bank. Examples include Bitcoin and Ethereum.

- **DAO (Decentralized Autonomous Organization):** An organization governed by rules encoded in smart contracts on a blockchain, enabling transparent and democratic decision-making.

- **DApp (Decentralized Application):** An application that runs on a decentralized network, such as a blockchain, rather than on a single, centralized server.

- **DeFi (Decentralized Finance):** A blockchain-based financial ecosystem offering services such as lending, borrowing, trading, and insurance without relying on traditional intermediaries.

- **DEX (Decentralized Exchange):** A platform that allows users to trade cryptocurrencies directly with each other without a centralized intermediary.

- **Gas:** A fee paid for executing transactions or smart contracts on certain blockchains, particularly Ethereum.

- **Hot Wallet:** A cryptocurrency wallet connected to the internet, offering convenience but slightly higher security risks.

- **Layer 2 scaling solutions:** Technologies built on top of existing blockchains to increase transaction speed and reduce fees.

- **Mining:** The process of verifying transactions and adding new blocks to a blockchain, often rewarded with cryptocurrency.

- **NFT (Non-Fungible Token):** A unique digital asset on a blockchain that represents ownership of items such as art, music, in-game assets, or collectibles.

- **Private Key:** A cryptographic key used for secure transactions on a blockchain that must be kept secret. It's like a highly secure password for your cryptocurrency.

- **Public Key:** A cryptographic key used for secure transactions on a blockchain that acts as your address for receiving cryptocurrency.

- **Regulation:** Government rules and laws that oversee the cryptocurrency and decentralized finance space.

- **Sharding:** A technique for dividing a blockchain network into smaller "shards" to improve efficiency and scalability.

- **Smart Contract:** A self-executing computer program on a blockchain that automates agreements and transactions, eliminating the need for intermediaries.

- **Stablecoin:** A type of cryptocurrency designed to maintain a stable value, often pegged to a real-world asset like the US dollar.

- **Token:** A digital asset issued on a blockchain, often used to represent ownership, utility, or participation within decentralized platforms.

- **Wallet:** A software application or hardware device used to store, send, and receive cryptocurrencies.

- **Web3:** The next generation of the internet, envisioning a decentralized and user-owned web powered by blockchain, cryptocurrencies, and other decentralized technologies.

- **Yield Farming:** A strategy in DeFi where users provide liquidity to protocols and earn rewards in the form of new tokens.

www.ingramcontent.com/pod-product-compliance
Lightning Source LLC
LaVergne TN
LVHW041222050326
832903LV00021B/756